# the
# SELF-PORTRAIT
# in
# art

# the
# SELF-PORTRAIT
# in
# art

By Sharon Lerner, Designed by Robert Clark Nelson ■ Lerner Publications Company, Minneapolis, Minnesota

*William Hogarth, Self-Portrait (1758); National Portrait Gallery, London.*

# Contents

*Jean Auguste Ingres, Portrait of the Artist as a Young Man; The Metropolitan Museum of Art, Bequest of Grace Rainey Rogers, 1943.*

# Introduction

Name any artist. You can almost be sure that he has made a self-portrait at one time or another. An artist creates from personal experience, familiar situations, to solve problems and to gain insight. A self-portrait can be the result of any one of these endeavors.

There is one model who is always available for an artist to paint. That is himself. He does not have to pay a model to sit for him. He does not have to go to a distant spot carrying heavy equipment. All he needs is a mirror. If he wants to practice a new technique, if he wants to study the structure of an eye or an ear, if he wants to record a smile or a scowl, he can always study his own face.

Some self-portraits are simple drawings, some are elaborate paintings. Some self-portraits are exact likenesses, some are images of what the artist would like to be, and some are pictures of how the artist thinks others see him. Sometimes an artist will picture himself in different roles—a wealthy prince, a pious saint, or a broken old man. The self-portrait is to an artist what an autobiography is to a writer, the opportunity to speak about himself.

Selection from the wealth of self-portraits available was difficult. Rembrandt made more than 100 self-portraits, and Cezanne painted nearly 40. We have included the most interesting, important and expressive ones, but remember this book is just an introduction.

*Parmigianino, Self-Portrait on a Convex Mirror (1523); Kunsthistorischen Museum, Vienna.*

*Lorenzo Ghiberti, Self-Portrait, Gates of Paradise (about 1450);*
*The Baptistery, Florence; Photo Alinari.*

## LORENZO GHIBERTI
### *1378-1455*

Look at this leprechaun of a man peering out at us. It is a sculptured self-portrait of Lorenzo Ghiberti (ghee-BEAR-tee). The head is part of the decoration on the East bronze doors of the Baptistery in Florence, Italy. This is a building near the Cathedral that was used for baptismal ceremonies.

A contest was held in Florence to select the best design for the North door of this building, and Ghiberti won. He started on that bronze door in 1403. It took him 21 years to complete the work. His achievement was so well-liked that he was asked to do the East door, too. The second door took another 22 years to complete.

The East door is divided into ten panels. Each one shows a different scene from the Old Testament. The sculpture is raised from a flat surface, a technique called *relief sculpture.* Around these panels are many small statues of Biblical figures and portraits of important citizens of Florence. One of these portraits is that of Ghiberti himself. It is only a few inches high, but we feel we know the man and his sense of humor, from this little self-portrait.

Michelangelo Buonarroti, (me-kel-AN-jay-lo bwo-nah-RO-tee) who was born in Florence 20 years after Ghiberti died, once said, "These doors are so beautiful that they could be the gates of Paradise". People agreed. To this day the doors are called by that name.

*Sandro Botticelli, Detail from Adoration of the Magi (1476); Uffizi Gallery, Florence; Photo Alinari.*

# ALESSANDRO BOTTICELLI
## *1444/5-1510*

When Sandro Botticelli (SAN-dro bot-tee-CHEL-lee) was born he was named Alessandro Filipepi. His older brother, who was very chubby, had been given the nickname Botticelli or "the little barrel". The name rubbed off on Sandro, too.

Botticelli was one of the leading artists of the early Italian *Renaissance,* which started in Italy in the 15th century. The Renaissance was a rebirth of the Greek and Roman spirit of scholarship and creativity. Great strides were made in art, science and literature. Lorenzo de Medici, (luh-REN-ZO MED-i-chee) the brilliant ruler of Florence and patron of the arts, helped to establish the Renaissance by commissioning gifted artists and writers to work for him. Botticelli painted several pictures for Lorenzo.

A wealthy banker asked Botticelli to paint a large picture showing the visit of the three kings for the Church of Santa Maria Novella.

Hoping to impress Lorenzo de Medici, the banker requested that the kings be portrayed as Lorenzo's father and brothers. Botticelli also painted other important Florentines on the canvas and in the one corner of the picture shown here he painted himself. Painting one's self-portrait in a large group picture was not uncommon. Botticelli is dressed in a gold cloak and is the only figure gazing directly out of the picture. He didn't sign this canvas. His gaze seems to attract your attention. Perhaps he wants to say, "I've signed this picture with my portrait".

Botticelli's favorite subjects were religious and mythological stories. His paintings are rich with pattern and detail. The women Botticelli painted are especially beautiful, but usually sad-eyed. The most delightful picture he did was the *Birth of Venus*. It shows Venus, the beautiful Goddess of Love, gliding across the sea in a large shell.

*Leonardo da Vinci, Self-Portrait (about 1510); Royal Library, Turin; Photo Alinari.*

# LEONARDO DA VINCI
## *1452-1519*

There are only six paintings by Leonardo da Vinci (lay-oh-NAR-doh duh-VEEN-chee) to see today. Yet he is considered one of the greatest artists ever to have lived. This self-portrait can help us understand why. The drawing, done in red chalk, makes us almost feel the wrinkled skin and long beard. We see a wise man with searching eyes and determined lips.

Leonardo was an inventor, an architect and a scientist, as well as an artist. Some historians have said he was a man born ahead of his time. Only a small number of his ideas were actually developed during his lifetime. They forecast many technical and scientific achievements of later ages.

Leonardo was unusually precise and exact in recording his various ideas, scientific observations and proposed inventions. He made detailed drawings and described his findings in *mirror writing* in his notebooks. (Da Vinci was left-handed and wrote backwards, so his writing could only be read with a mirror.)

He was curious about the flight of birds and would sit for hours sketching their movements as they soared and glided. He decided that man could fly if he had proper wings, and built a huge pair out of wood and cloth. The wings were to be strapped to a man's shoulders and flapped by a set of foot-pedals. Naturally they were unsuccessful, but they demonstrate Leonardo's interest in aerodynamics and the principles of flight in an age when other men did not think about these things. His notebooks also contain plans for planes similar to gliders and helicopters.

Leonardo studied the movement of air and water. He liked to wander near the ocean and watch the waves as they came in and out. He was fascinated by plants and how they grew. He discovered that leaves are naturally arranged so that each one gets its share of sunlight. He studied the structure of the human body and the working of muscles. He made notes and drawings of the development and growth of an unborn baby.

Dukes and Princes called on him to design palaces, military equipment, weapons, bridges and sewage systems. He designed the first armored tank and the first movable bridge. Leonardo's plan for an underground sewage system was completely new. In his time cities were very dirty and disease-ridden. Garbage and sewage were just thrown into the streets.

Leonardo experimented a great deal with paints. Unfortunately, many of these experiments were unsuccessful. The colors chipped or faded and the paintings were lost. As a result, we have very few paintings remaining by Leonardo the artist. Of these, The *Last Supper* and *Mona Lisa* are the most famous.

Mona Lisa was not a beautiful woman but her expression fascinated Leonardo. He liked his painting of her so much that he would not part with it. He painted this famous portrait while musicians played soft music and a reader recited poetry. Mona Lisa sat quietly with her hands folded, listening. A mysterious smile played around her mouth and eyes. The secret of the smile and the beauty of the painting lie in the mellowed colors and blurred outlines that make one part merge with another. This technique, which leaves something to your imagination, is called *sfumato* (sfew-MAH-toh) and was one of Leonardo's many developments.

# MICHELANGELO BUONARROTI
## *1475-1564*

Michelangelo Buonarroti was an extraordinary man, who lived at the same time as Leonardo da Vinci. These two brought art and the quest for knowledge to that peak we now call the *High Renaissance*. Michelangelo was a brilliant sculptor, painter, architect and poet. But he was a lonely man. He had few friends. Wealth, luxuries and fine clothes meant nothing to him. He cared only for his work. Everything he did was on a grand scale and done with deep concentration. He undertook the most difficult assignments, and achieved the greatest art.

As a boy of 14, Michelangelo was apprenticed to an important Florentine painter. Soon the beauty of his work surpassed that of his teacher's. But in spite of his skill, Michelangelo was not interested in painting. He wanted to be a sculptor. Lorenzo de Medici was impressed by his talent and became his patron. Thereafter Michelangelo lived in the Medici palace where he met and talked with the most influential men of the Renaissance.

Lorenzo had a fine collection of ancient Greek and Roman sculpture, which Michelangelo was able to study. He saw that the ancient sculptors had a thorough knowledge of the human body. A figure carved in the round could be seen from every angle, and movement of one part affected the whole body.

Michelangelo knew that he would have to study *anatomy,* or structure of the body. Studying plaster casts and models was not enough to teach him the positions of the bones and how the muscles worked. But at that time in Florence it was forbidden to dissect the human body. Michelangelo's desire proved stronger than the law. Despite the risk, he would secretly perform dissections. Very slowly and carefully, tissue by tissue, he cut, marveling at the construction and design of the body.

This careful study was translated into many magnificent sculptures, among them the powerful statue of *David*. The large pillar of marble from which the *David* was made had a flaw, and no other sculptor would consider it. But Michelangelo worked around the flaw in a way that made it useful. Sculpting in marble thrilled and excited Michelangelo. By chiseling and carving, he was awakening a figure which was asleep in the stone. He worked with vigor and concentration from light to dark, often not stopping to eat or rest. Marble dust filled his nose and made him cough, but he hardly noticed. Slowly life awoke in the marble.

Almost all of Michelangelo's work was done by request of a pope, cardinal or nobleman. Pope Julius II asked Michelangelo to decorate the ceiling of the Sistine Chapel with *frescos,* or paintings in wet plaster. Michelangelo was enraged. He was a sculptor, not a painter! But a commission from the Pope had to be honored. From 1508 to 1512 he worked at covering the 10,000 square feet of the ceiling with stories from the Bible—the Creation, Moses and the Prophets. Lying on his back on a scaffolding 60 feet above the floor, he painted 343 figures, 225 of them ranging from 10 to 18 feet high. The figures have the monumental look of sculpture. They are charged with life and emotion.

Between 1548 and 1555, at about the same time that he was designing and supervising the building of the magnificent dome of St. Peter's Cathedral in Rome, Michelangelo sculpted the white marble statue you see here. It shows Jesus after he was taken off the cross. The old man standing over Jesus, holding him, is Nicodemus, and the two women are Mary and Mary Magdalen. The strength and dignity of this work is a tribute to Michelangelo's genius. Its tenderness and reality make you want to watch to see if indeed the figures are not breathing.

The face of Nicodemus is a self-portrait of Michelangelo. Here is a reverent, sad old man, bearded and with a broken nose. Michelangelo was always troubled by his nose, which had been broken in his youth by a jealous artist friend. It never healed properly and often caused him pain. Michelangelo had wanted this statue to stand at his grave, but instead it is now in the Cathedral of Florence.

Raphael (RAH-fah-el) came to Florence in 1504. He had been an apprentice painter in Urbino. When he arrived, Michelangelo's magnificent sculpture of *David* had just been placed in front of the city hall, and the paint had scarcely dried on Leonardo da Vinci's *Mona Lisa*. With gifted artists like da Vinci and Michelangelo at work, art standards were very high and artists were competing for commissions.

Raphael was a hard worker. Before he began to paint a picture he made countless sketches, searching for the perfect pose and the correct relationship of each figure. Soon Raphael's paintings became known for their balanced compositions, calm beauty and sweet-faced madonnas. Usually his madonnas were not painted from models, but from the artist's imagination. In each he pictured his personal idea of beauty and grace.

Raphael was a very good-natured and sociable man. He enjoyed great popularity and lived in a grand style equalled by few artists before or after him. Popes and princes were his friends. There was even talk that he might be made a Cardinal.

Raphael was a man of many artistic achievements and interests. He studied the ruins of ancient Rome and designed several buildings. He painted many portraits, large frescos and murals. Pope Julius II asked Raphael to decorate the walls and ceilings of several rooms in the Vatican with frescos. He worked on them at the same time that Michelangelo was painting his famous frescos in the Sistine Chapel, another part of the Vatican.

Raphael died on his 37th birthday. This self-portrait was painted a few years earlier. The eyes are the most interesting part of the picture. Finely shaped, large and still, they take in everything at a glance. The eyes of the artist are *seeing* eyes, trained to absorb and store away images and color.

## RAPHAEL SANZIO
### *1483-1520*

*Raphael, Self-Portrait (about 1518); Uffizi Gallery, Florence; Photo Alinari.*

# ALBRECHT DÜRER
## *1471-1528*

When Albrecht Dürer (AHL-brekt DYOOR-er) was 13 years old he sat in front of a mirror and made this silver point drawing of himself. He drew with a special pencil that had a silver tip and made grey lines. The silver pencil was the drawing pencil of the past. Our *graphite,* or lead pencil is an invention of the 20th century. Dürer sketched and shaded his face and long hair very carefully because he knew the fine lines made by the silver pencil would not erase. The delicate nose and almond eyes show a serious boy, eager to do well. He drew only one hand and hid the other in his sleeve. Drawing hands was difficult even for Dürer! Many years after this sketch was completed the artist wrote in the corner of his very first self-portrait, "This portrait of myself I drew from my reflection in a mirror, in the year 1484, when I was yet a child."

Dürer made many other self-portraits during his life. Drawing was a way of speaking for him. He once drew a sketch of his body for the doctor and pointed out the exact location of a pain.

Dürer was born in Nuremberg, Germany, the son of a goldsmith who wanted him to follow the same trade. But Dürer chose to be an artist and went to study in the studio of the best-known painter of his hometown.

Like all young artists, Dürer yearned to travel. He wanted to see the work of his contemporaries, and the work of the past. His journeys took him through Germany, Switzerland, and Italy. Wherever he went he sketched mountains and trees, and produced watercolors of quaint towns.

Dürer was greatly influenced by Italian art and the Renaissance search for beauty. At that time Italian artists paid a great deal of attention to composition and perspective. German artists emphasized details. Dürer combined these styles in his own work. He helped to bring Renaissance ideals to northern Europe.

After Dürer's travels he set up a studio in Nuremberg. He was kept very busy with commissions. His drawings, engravings and woodcuts are seldom equalled in their beauty and clarity. His work covers a wide range of subjects—devils and saints, landscapes and portraits. Dürer's sketch books are filled with studies of cats, birds and other animals. He studied nature down to the smallest details. His famous watercolor of a rabbit shows every soft hair of its furry coat and each twitching whisker.

Many artists at this time did not sign their work. But Dürer signed many of his nearly 100 paintings, more than 1,000 drawings and nearly 100 woodcuts and engravings with his special monogram. The A for Albrecht fits perfectly over the D for Dürer.

*Albrecht Dürer, Self-Portrait (1484); Albertina, Vienna.*

# HANS HOLBEIN
## the Younger
### *1497-1543*

Hans Holbein (HOLE-bine) the Younger and Albrecht Dürer are considered the outstanding figures of German art. Holbein was born in Augsburg into a family of artists. His brothers, nephew and father, Hans Holbein the Elder, were all painters.

As a young man Holbein went to live in Basle, Switzerland. There his talent as a designer, book illustrator, wood engraver and portrait painter developed. Holbein had a keen sense of humor. Once he painted a letter, eyeglasses, a quill and ink on a tabletop. These objects looked so real that people tried to pick them up. Such tricks delighted Holbein.

At that time religious influence in Switzerland repressed interest in the arts. In 1526 Holbein went to London. Sir Thomas More, a powerful English statesman and writer, became his patron and friend. Holbein was appointed painter to the court of Henry VIII. As such he designed jewelry, furniture, costumes for pageants and decorations for halls. But his most important job was to paint portraits of the Tudor king and his royal family. Henry VIII said, "I could make six peers (noblemen) out of six ploughmen (peasants), but out of six peers I could not make one Holbein."

Portrait painting was Holbein's greatest achievement. Before he started a portrait he made many careful drawings or studies of the person he was painting. It wasn't unusual for a sitter to sit three to five hours a day for several weeks while Holbein slowly produced a lifelike portrait with remarkable honesty and detail. Because of his keen observations we have vivid pictures of the people of Henry VIII's time.

Unfortunately, to our knowledge, Holbein left no painted portrait of himself. This colored drawing was done one year before his death. In it we see a rather handsome and strong face and the artist's inspecting eyes. It is a straight-forward and realistic portrait. But it doesn't show the interesting details that make Holbein's paintings so outstanding.

In the year 1543 the Plague, or Black Death, swept London. One of its first victims was Hans Holbein, the Younger. He was 46 years old when he died.

# PIETER BRUEGHEL
## the Elder
### *1525-1569*

This drawing by Pieter Brueghel (PEE-ter BREW-gul) the Elder shows the artist finishing a painting as the buyer looks over his shoulder. Observe the penetrating eyes and firm mouth of the artist, and then look at the very different, narrow eyes and thin, parted lips of the buyer. Two distinct personalities are portrayed. Brueghel's careful drawing even shows the crude hand sewing on his coat. Do you suppose the buyer is holding money to purchase the picture in the bag closed in his fist?

Brueghel is best remembered for his realistic scenes of Flemish peasants feasting, merrymaking and working. Brueghel's colorful pictures are alive with people, activity and detail. They show how the 16th century farmer lived and looked in Flanders, a country which included parts of what is now modern Belgium and northern France. Pictures that portray daily life are called *genre* (ZHAHN-ruh) paintings.

Brueghel's paintings are very well organized. His busy scenes of large groups of people are not confusing or over-crowded. He carefully planned the placement and character of each figure. Bright, gay and contrasting colors are dominant.

Because Brueghel painted peasants, it is sometimes assumed that he was a peasant. He was actually an educated townsman and lived in the big cities of Antwerp and Brussels. In common with the northern European artists of his day, Brueghel went to Italy to study. Although the style of the time was to paint religious and mythological subjects, Brueghel preferred to paint the peasants he knew and understood. Unfortunately less than 50 of his paintings still exist.

Brueghel had several sons. The oldest and youngest were also painters. The oldest, Pieter Brueghel the Younger (1564-1638), was known as "Hell" Brueghel because of the horrible nightmare-like scenes he painted. The youngest, Jan "Velvet" Brueghel (1568-1625), painted very refined and delicate pictures of flowers. Brueghel the Elder died soon after his sons were born, and so he did not train them in their work. But Pieter Brueghel the Younger made many copies of his father's paintings. Neither son attained the world fame of their father.

*Pieter Brueghel, Self-Portrait with Buyer; Albertina, Vienna.*

We know little about the life of El Greco (el GREK-oh). He left no diary, only his art. The information we have was gathered in bits and pieces from city records, writings and legend. We do know that he was born on the Greek island of Crete and named Domenikos Theotocopoulos. El Greco is Spanish for "the Greek". The nickname was given to him when he lived in Spain and has stuck with him through the centuries.

As a young man, El Greco left Crete and travelled to Venice to study the works of Venetian masters, Titian (TISH-un) and Tintoretto (tin-toe-RET-oh). Then he went to Rome to see Michelangelo's paintings in the Sistine Chapel. He finally settled in the gloomy town of Toledo, Spain.

The religious climate of late 16th century Spain appealed to the devout Greek artist. He wanted to portray the saints and illustrate the stories of the Church. El Greco's paintings are characterized by unnaturally long, disjointed figures which seem to reach toward heaven. Thunder and lightning surround his figures and give power to his canvases.

**EL GRECO**
*1541-1614*

El Greco was not a popular artist in his day. People didn't take to his daring technique and religious *ecstasy,* or intensely emotional quality. He was forgotten after his death. His work was rediscovered and called great in the late 19th century.

As far as we know, El Greco never stated that this picture was his self-portrait. But art historians agree that it must be one. The experts base their reasoning on the likeness of this and another El Greco portrait. The canvas here shows an old and tired man. A much earlier painting shows a young man with the same face. Who but the artist himself would serve twice as a model at an interval of about 40 years?

*Peter Paul Rubens, The Artist and Isabella Brandt (1609); Alte Pinakothek, Munich.*

## PETER PAUL RUBENS
### *1577-1640*

Peter Paul Rubens, one of the greatest of all Flemish painters, did this double portrait soon after his marriage to Isabella Brandt. She wears a mischievous smile and her head is cupped in a splendid ruff. Their beautiful clothes tell us that they are well-to-do. Rubens portrayed himself and Isabella as a contented and happy couple enjoying their prosperity. This is an early painting, and it only hints at the robust style Rubens was to perfect a few years later.

When Rubens got old he suffered with a crippled hand. Some days it was so painful that he could not paint. When he was 62, one year before his death, he painted the self-portrait on the next page showing himself wearing a black velvet cloak. His once-elegant hand is covered by a glove and rests on a cane. Rubens' face is heavier but still handsome. His sad eyes show suffering, yet they are proud eyes of a true artist.

It is interesting to compare these two paintings. You can see how Rubens' style changed in 30 years. In the later portrait he paid less attention to details of lace and jewels, and gave us a full impression of his personality—perhaps a personality which had become more interested in character than in finery.

Rubens lived a full life. He began his career by studying painting and drawing in Antwerp. His teachers taught him all they could

# RUBENS

and then encouraged him to go to Italy. He stayed in Italy eight years, marvelling at the work of the Renaissance artists and painting altarpieces for cardinals and noblemen. When he was 31 he returned to Antwerp. The Archduke Albert, ruler of Flanders, welcomed him home and asked him to be his court painter. Rubens was paid a huge salary and built himself a beautiful villa.

He opened a studio in Antwerp and soon had so many commissions that he had to hire assistants to help him get the work done. Two of his most talented assistants were Anthony Van Dyck (Van DIKE) and Jan Brueghel. Usually Rubens would plan and paint a small sketch, and then his assistants would transfer the idea to a big canvas and paint in the first outlines. Rubens himself would paint the major parts and important details. With a few brushstrokes he could give life to a picture.

Rubens' religious and mythological pictures, landscapes, portraits and genre paintings all have a great deal of drama, vitality and movement. Nothing seems still in a Rubens painting. The figures appear to be breathing. His efforts contributed a great deal toward bringing the Renaissance to northern Europe. Rubens was the most famous painter of his time, and painted about 500 pictures during his life. Commissions poured into his studio from all over Europe. He painted for Louis XIII of France, for Louis' mother Maria de Medici, for Philip III of Spain, and for Charles I of England, who made him a knight. When travelling from court to court as an honored guest, he often served as an ambassador. Rubens was a very charming man and an expert at handling delicate political matters. He spoke six languages, and his clever negotiations helped to keep peace between England and Spain.

# ANTHONY VAN DYCK
## *1599-1641*

This self-portrait is an *etching*. The very fine lines and specks which make up the face of Anthony Van Dyck are characteristic of etchings. The word itself comes from a German word meaning to eat or corrode. In an etching the picture is scratched into a wax-covered metal plate. The plate is put into an acid bath which eats into the metal only where the wax has been scratched away. Then the wax is removed. Ink is wiped over the plate and catches in the grooves made by the acid. The inked plate is then printed on moist paper in a press. One of the advantages of an etching is that many copies of the same picture can be made.

Do you think Van Dyck forgot to finish this portrait? More likely he left it this way intentionally. The large area of white makes a very interesting contrast to the fine black details of the head. Van Dyck has portrayed himself in a curious pose. He must have been looking over his shoulder into a mirror placed behind him. The object of the pose might be to give the feeling that his work had been interrupted. Annoyed, he seems to be looking around for the disturbance.

Anthony Van Dyck was born in Antwerp, the son of a wealthy silk merchant. As a young man he became an assistant to Peter Paul Rubens. Some of Van Dyck's early paintings closely follow the grand style of Rubens. To this day, experts have a difficult time telling which artist painted certain of the works done while they were in the same studio.

An acquaintance described Van Dyck, saying, "He behaved more like a noble than like an ordinary burgher (townsman). Following a practice acquired from Rubens he wore magnificent clothes. His cap and dress he decked with feathers and precious stones; around his neck hung a golden chain, and servants followed him about, so that everyone turned and stared at him."

Van Dyck's fame as a portrait artist spread through Europe. He made portraits of the rich and titled, painting them not so much as they really looked, but more as they wished to look. He was not interested in portraying personality or character but chose instead to show elegance, beauty and fashion. King Charles I of England asked him to be his court painter, and Van Dyck's greatest masterpiece is a large portrait of Charles I with his horse. The painting now hangs in Paris at the Louvre.

*Anthony Van Dyck, The Artist; Courtesy, Museum of Fine Arts, Boston.*

*Rembrandt Van Rijn, Self-Portrait (1640); National Gallery, London.*

# REMBRANDT VAN RIJN
## *1606-1669*

Rembrandt Van Rijn (REM-brant van RINE) left no notebooks or diaries recording the thoughts and events of his life. But he did leave an autobiography—a visual one—in the form of more than 100 self-portraits. Seventy paintings, about 30 etchings and a few drawings spanning 40 years speak to us about this great Dutch artist's life. Many of the early ones show Rembrandt elegantly dressed in silks and velvets studded with jewels. Later ones are character studies of a man of many moods. Some are simple facial sketches done of himself for lack of any other model.

These two self-portraits were painted 20 years apart and under very different circumstances. The first one shows a richly dressed, successful and confident young man of 34. At that time Rembrandt was the foremost portrait painter of Amsterdam with more commissions than he could handle. He, his attractive wife Saskia and their children lived extravagantly in a big house filled with a collection of Italian paintings and other treasures. The second picture shows Rembrandt at the age of 53. Here is a tired old man who has lost his wife and several children. Financial troubles have forced him to sell his house and collection of paintings at a public auction. Rembrandt was still considered a gifted artist, but his style was no longer popular. It is interesting that some of the paintings now considered his best were done at this time.

You can see how two decades changed his style. The later portrait is a thoughtful character study done in a rather rough style with more interest in personality than

*Rembrandt Van Rijn, Self-Portrait (1659); National Gallery of Art, Washington, D. C., Mellon Collection.*

precision. The earlier one is painted with emphasis on fashion, beauty and detail.

These portraits show the artist's careful scrutiny of his own features as he tried to reveal himself to us. We are brought face to face with a real man. In each painting the interplay of light and shadow draws our attention to the head, which is alive and expressive. This technique was marvelously perfected by Rembrandt.

Rembrandt had the great gift of being able to express with a brush, pen or etching needle what the eye can see and the heart can feel. His biblical scenes, portraits and landscapes, are dramatic, sad, gay and romantic. But all are very beautiful. We are fortunate that he left us more than 700 paintings, 300 etchings and 1,000 drawings.

The painter with his back to us is Jan Vermeer (ver-MARE). In this unique self-portrait Vermeer shows himself at work in his studio. If we look over his shoulders we see him carefully painting the model's hat. There is a strange stillness about Vermeer's painting. The figures don't stir, yet they are full of life. Notice how the model is bathed in a glow of light from a window behind the curtain. One small picture similar to the one on the easel might have taken Vermeer months to complete. His works are masterpieces of color, light and detail.

The interesting map on the wall, the brocaded curtain, tiled floor and assorted objects make a fascinating background. If you look at his other paintings you will find that he has repeated some of these furnishings.

Vermeer's full name was Jan Vermeer Van Delft. It means Jan Vermeer of the city of Delft. The artist spent his whole life in Delft, a city of canals and windmills, important for the manufacture of china dishes. Vermeer was a popular artist and his works sold at high prices. But he enjoyed luxuries, and he had a large family. As a result of his high expenses he died a poor man.

Only about 40 paintings by Vermeer are known to us, yet he ranks along with Rembrandt as one of the greatest artists of Holland. Their excellence and their scarcity make his paintings among the world's most valuable. Vermeer is famous for beautifully painted scenes of Dutch 17th century life.

### JAN VERMEER VAN DELFT
*1632-1675*

*Jan Vermeer, The Artist in his Studio (after 1670); Kunsthistorischen Museum, Vienna*

*Sir Joshua Reynolds, Self-Portrait (1748); National Portrait Gallery, London.*

# JOSHUA REYNOLDS
## *1723-1792*

Joshua Reynolds painted more than 2,000 portraits. Children were his favorite subjects. His portraits of adults were done in the elegant style of Van Dyck. They were flattering likenesses, showing the model at his very best. This was what wealthy 18th century Englishmen wanted, and this was what Reynolds gave them. Reynolds believed that by being grand and beautiful, art became great.

This self-portrait shows Reynolds at age 25, near the start of his career as one of England's foremost portrait artists. The young painter is pictured with his left hand shading his eyes and his right hand holding brushes and palette. Do you see the dark shadow of Reynolds' hand as it shades his face? The pose is very unusual. The artist seems to be deep in thought. A frown clouds his face. Perhaps he wanted to show us himself as he studies an unfinished painting, deciding where to place the next stroke. Notice the condition of the surface of the painting. When oil paint grows old it often cracks.

# ELIZABETH VIGÉE LE BRUN
## *1755-1842*

Vigée Le Brun (vee-zhay luh brun) is one of the few women artists of her time still remembered today. She was born in Paris, the daughter of an artist. By the age of 15 she had already developed a skillful technique and acquired a wide reputation. Having one's portrait painted by this beautiful and talented girl was popular with the French nobility, especially the women. She painted with a woman's eye, and like Reynolds and Van Dyck, showed her subjects at their fashionable best. She painted Queen Marie Antoinette's portrait many times. The two women were friends and liked to sing duets.

In 1789 the long and bloody French Revolution began. Friends of royalty like Vigée Le Brun were not safe in Paris. She and her young daughter fled to Italy dressed as workers, leaving unfinished paintings behind.

Her fine reputation as a painter had spread before her. Everywhere Vigée Le Brun went, people welcomed her and commissioned her to paint. She moved as an exile from one country to another for many years. Finally, tired of wandering, she returned home to Napoleon's France to live out her life.

When she was in Florence, the Uffizi (oo-FEET-see) Gallery asked her to paint this self-portrait. It became part of the Uffizi's large and unique collection of self-portraits. It shows the artist at the age of 35. The head is exquisitely painted and shows Vigée Le Brun's beauty and good nature. The dark dress and white cap were her painting clothes. Compare the different textures the artist shows in her lace collar and satin sash. There is a thin, delicate, almost transparent feeling in the lace, and a heavy, stiff and shiny quality in the satin. The effect is so real that you want to touch the fabric. Notice the crude paintbrushes in her hand. A tuft of fur or hair was tied to a stick for a brush.

Vigée Le Brun was devoted to her art. She wrote, "To paint and to live are the same to me."

# FRANCISCO DE GOYA
## *1746-1828*

Here is an unusual portrait of two men. One is terribly sick and weak, and the other is strong and self-assured. The helpless man is Francisco Goya (GO-yah) and the other is his faithful friend, Doctor **Arrieta** (ARE-ree-et-TA). The picture was painted in muted shades of brown, red and violet, with a few strong highlights. These colors create an atmosphere of suffering. The contrast between the pale, exhausted face of Goya, and the calm, healthy face of the doctor brings out the graveness of Goya's illness. Dr. **Arrieta** steadies Goya into a sitting position to take a glass of medicine. Goya grasps at the sheets for support as the doctor urges him to drink. If you look very carefully you will see three blurred heads in the background. The one on the far left is a priest, next to him is probably Goya's cousin and housekeeper, and on the right is a very mysterious face with an open mouth. Perhaps this is the appearance of death.

Goya painted this frank and intimate self-portrait after he had recovered from his illness. He felt deeply indebted for Dr. **Arrieta**'s care, and wrote this inscription in Spanish at the bottom of the canvas: "Goya thanks his friend **Arrieta** for the sureness and care with which he saved his life from serious and dangerous illness suffered at the end of the year 1819 at the age of seventy-three. Painted in 1820."

Goya was born in a small Spanish village. He was a little boy when he began to draw with pieces of charcoal. A priest discovered his work and took him to Madrid to study, where he quickly became popular. He was known not only for his art work, but also for his skillful dancing and his love of a good time.

Goya, one of Spain's greatest artists, is remembered for both his etchings and paintings. Through Goya's work we see Spain of 150 years ago—the colorful bullfights, the terribly poor peasants, the glitter of the Spanish court and the horrors of the French occupation of Spain. Goya was skilled in expressing his ideas and feelings. In many etchings he depicts the sad side of human nature with fantastic witches, devils and giants. Truth and meaning were his aims, beauty was secondary to him.

King Charles IV made Goya his court painter. Charles and his royal Spanish family were known for their greed and corruption. Goya painted them in their expensive silks and sparkling jewels, but in their faces he showed the unmistakable look of boredom, vanity and even stupidity.

*Francisco Goya, Self-Portrait with Dr. Arrieta (1820); The Minneapolis Institute of Arts, Ethel Morrison Van Derlip Fund.*

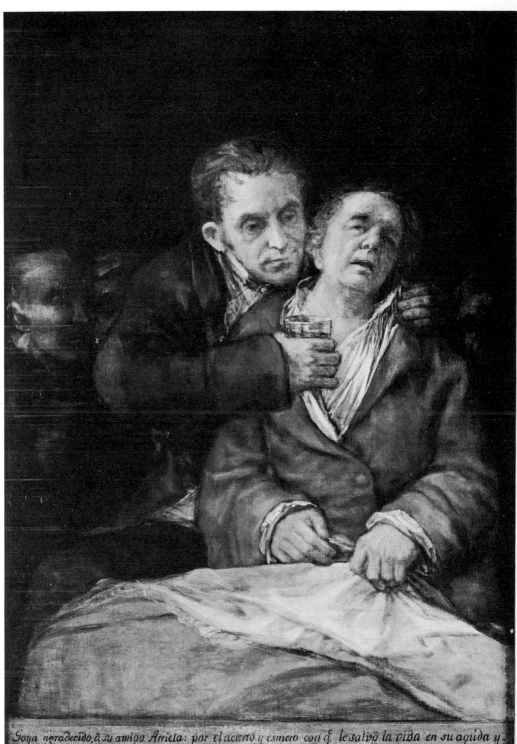

*Goya agradecido, à su amigo Arrieta: por el acierto y esmero con q.ͤ le salvó la vida en su aguda y peligrosa enfermedad, padecida à fines del año 1819. a los setenta y tres de su edad. Lo pintó en 1820.*

*John Singleton Copley, The Copley Family (1780); National Gallery of Art, Washington, D. C., Purchase Fund, Andrew W. Mellon gift.*

John Singleton Copley (COP-lee) was one of the most successful and talented artists in the American colonies. He was born in Boston, Massachusetts. As a boy he drew in the margins of his schoolbooks, and learned about painting while watching his artist stepfather at work.

At 13 the stepfather died and Copley was left head of his family. The young man turned to painting to support his mother and brother. In the colonies at that time painting was considered a useful trade requiring no more special skill, and with no more status, than shoemaking or carpentry. Few painters could make their living as artists. Most earned their bread painting signs or walls, and considered portrait and landscape painting their hobby. In spite of this, Copley worked hard teaching himself to draw and paint. Soon all of New England had heard of John Copley's portraits. He became one of the few artists with a busy studio. His paintings hung in Boston homes in wood frames carved by his friend, Paul Revere.

By the age of 35 Copley reached his peak as a painter. He had produced more than 275 pictures, and was a wealthy man with three houses and 20 acres on Beacon Hill. But he was restless, and in 1774, just before the start of the Revolutionary War, he sailed for Europe, never returning to America. He settled in England, and devoted himself to painting large historical scenes. Critics said his pictures had lost the honest realism that had made him great. In England he did not enjoy the fame he had in America.

This picture of Copley's family was one of his greatest achievements. The portrait shows Copley in the top left of the picture, with his father-in-law, wife, three daughters and son. Each member of the family is personally portrayed—the father-in-law with a stern look and white powdered wig, the sweet-faced, affectionate children, the understanding wife and the calm, almost bored-looking Copley. The family had to sit quietly for many hours while Copley captured their likenesses. The landscape they sit before was painted from a setting in the artist's studio. Copley paid great attention to details. Notice the ornate pattern on the rug and couch and the little doll and feathered hat in the corner. Do you think one of the children dropped them there, or did the artist need them for his composition?

### JOHN SINGLETON COPLEY
*1738-1815*

Friendly Indians introduced young Benjamin West to painting. They showed him how to mix the red and yellow clay they used to paint their faces. West's mother gave him blue dye. With red, yellow and blue, the primary colors, he found he could mix any color he wanted. A few hairs pulled from the family cat's tail and put through a goose quill made his first paint brush.

West was the son of a Quaker innkeeper. He was born in Springfield, Pennsylvania in the same year as Copley. By the time he was 12 years old he was selling his pictures to the neighbors. When he was 16, his work was known in towns two days' ride away. He was a successful portrait painter at 20.

West hoped to go to Europe to study. At this time in colonial America, artists dreamed of going abroad to see the great art of Europe. Part of a young painter's training was to know and understand the art of the past, but there were no art museums and few important paintings in America for artists to study. A group of wealthy Philadelphians who admired West's work paid for his trip to Italy.

## BENJAMIN WEST
### *1738-1820*

West went from Italy to London, where King George III became his patron. He was soon a successful painter of historical, mythological and religious pictures. His purpose in art was not to please the eye, but to lift the mind. He helped and taught many American artists who came to London to study. He was one of the founders of the English Royal Academy and became its second president. This was an unusual honor for an American artist.

West never returned to America, but he never forgot it. He longed for things American, and it is said that he planted the first Indian corn in England.

This self-portrait was done in London, when West was 32 years old. The artist is dressed in a blue-grey suit and large black hat. He seems to be thinking about what he will paint on the canvas he holds in his lap.

*Benjamin West, Self-Portrait (1770); National Gallery of Art, Washington, D. C., Mellon Collection.*

James Whistler was an eccentric man with a biting wit. He wore outlandish clothes designed by himself, and when he went out even his shoelaces had to harmonize with his suit. He carried a bamboo walking stick, and wore a monocle in his right eye. Nevertheless, he was a very serious, sensitive and dedicated artist.

Whistler was born in Lowell, Massachusetts. As a boy he lived in St. Petersburg, where his father helped build the first Russian railway. When he was 17 Whistler entered West Point, but was dropped out three years later because of poor grades in chemistry. Skilled in drawing, Whistler got a job as a mapmaker for the United States Government. He earned $1.50 a day. The idea of studying painting, however, intrigued him, and he left America at the age of 21 to settle in Europe.

In Paris, and later in London, Whistler developed his original painting style and philosophy. He felt art should appeal to the senses, not to the emotions. He believed that the subject matter of a painting was not so important as the manner in which the artist showed the subject and developed the composition and color. He gave his pictures such titles as *Harmony in Grey and Green* and *Nocturne in Black and Gold,* names that give no hint as to the subject. One of the world's most famous portraits he called *Arrangement in Grey and Black.* Whistler wanted to call the viewer's attention to the composition and use of color. But the public put the subject first. Most of us know this gentle profile as *Whistler's Mother.*

Whistler was influenced by Japanese art. In this curious self-portrait he borrowed the Oriental use of open space, subtle contrast and simplicity. He worked very hard to achieve his easy style of painting. The quick yet beautiful strokes that make up the ladies' gowns took special care and skill. The entire picture is done in the limited palette of rust, grey and white. The mustached Whistler stares strangely out of the picture. He seems unaware of the two women busily talking behind him.

## JAMES MacNEILL WHISTLER
### *1834-1903*

*James Whistler, The Artist in his Studio (1864); The Art Institute of Chicago, Friends of American Art Collection.*

# EDGAR DEGAS
## *1834-1917*

Edgar Degas (duh-gah) gazes out at us from this etched self-portrait. He was a short man, with large sensitive eyes and an untidy mustache and beard. He was known for his quick temper and sharp tongue. Degas did not marry. He said he was afraid a wife would interfer with his work. His art meant more than anything else to him. "When I haven't put in a couple of hours' hard work, I feel guilty, stupid and worthless," he once wrote to a friend.

Degas was the eldest son of a well-to-do Parisian banker. He studied law at his parents' request, but being a lawyer didn't interest him, and he finally decided to become an artist. First he studied in Paris and then went to Italy to see the works of the Old Masters. The religious and mythological paintings of the Renaissance left him unsatisfied. He wanted to paint from his own experience. Degas was fascinated with the people of Paris. Musicians, jockeys, milliners, washerwomen, ballet dancers and singers were his favorite subjects. Sitting unnoticed in a corner of a ballet studio or in a millinery shop, he would busily sketch, catching his models off guard and in natural poses. Degas' pictures give the feeling that he spied on his subjects through a keyhole.

Before starting a painting Degas carefully planned his pictures by making many drawings and color notes of his subject. He was not completely satisfied with the effects of oil paint, and he experimented with other media. He liked the color and textural qualities of *pastel,* a soft colored chalk. Many of Degas' most beautiful and best-known works are done in pastel. Near the end of his life, his eyesight started to fail and he turned to sculpting figures in clay and wax.

# PIERRE AUGUSTE RENOIR
## *1841-1919*

Pierre Renoir (run-wahr) was born in Limoges, France. He was the son of a tailor and one of a large family. At 13 he went to work in a Parisian studio decorating china dishes, but lost his job when a mechanical method of painting was introduced. To earn a living he turned to decorating window shades and fans. Meanwhile he attended art classes at night to improve his drawing. By the time Renoir was 21 years old he had decided on a career as an artist.

Renoir and some artist friends often went to the beautiful forest area of Fontainbleau to paint. In the evenings they would go to a small cafe called Mother Anthony's to eat and drink. This picture is named *Le Caberet de la Mere Anthony.* It shows Renoir, standing, and two of his friends, just after finishing a meal. Nana, the waitress, is clearing the table and Toto, the white poodle, is resting on the floor. Toto had a wooden leg, but you cannot see it in the picture. The woman with a handkerchief around her hair and her back to us is Mother Anthony. The walls of the cafe are covered with drawings made by the many artists who lived in the area. This painting was one of Renoir's first important works. He always said, "It is one of the pictures I like most to remember." The characteristic style he developed later is only hinted at here.

Renoir was one of a group of French artists who were known as *Impressionists.* The Impressionists were interested in color and light. They painted their colorful and shimmering pictures out-of-doors in order to make the best use of natural light. They used quick, short brushstrokes. The Impressionist gives his impression or feelings about a scene in blurred hues and forms, and your eye brings the colors and shapes into focus. Renoir painted many pictures in this style. But after a trip to Italy and his discovery of the work of the Renaissance masters, he modified his technique. Renoir took the best of Impressionism—its color and vividness, and the best of Renaissance style—its design and form, and combined them into his own style. He painted mostly women, children and flowers in gay, rich color. His favorite color, red, is seen in almost all his work.

During the last 20 years of his life Renoir suffered from arthritis. Towards the end his condition was so bad that he could only paint with his brushes tied to his hands. But he never stopped painting as long as he lived.

*Pierre Renoir, Le Cabaret de la Mere Anthony (1866); National Museum, Stockholm.*

Paul Gauguin (go gan) was a successful Parisian stockbroker, husband and father of five. He taught himself to paint and enjoyed painting on Sundays. But this life did not satisfy him. Gauguin wanted to paint everyday. At the age of 35, he left his family and career to paint and wander in faraway places.

Gauguin felt that the values of Western civilization were wrong. The industrial society of the time made men greedy for money. He felt that artists were not expressing themselves honestly. To get away from false values, Gauguin went to live among the peasants of Brittany, in western France. The honesty of the peasants impressed him, and his paintings took on the simple look of folk art.

Another lonely painter was also working in the peaceful countryside. Vincent Van Gogh (van-GO) invited Gauguin to live and paint with him. Both men were hot-tempered and stubborn. They disagreed violently about painting, arguing over the smallest detail. In a fit of madness Van Gogh tried to kill Gauguin. Their friendship ended, and Gauguin went back to Paris.

Still searching for a simple life, Gauguin went to the South Pacific island of Tahiti. He lived as a native and painted his new friends there. He painted in strong, bright colors, sometimes using them in an unrealistic way. He might paint blue mountains and a red sky. Usually he outlined his figures to make them stand out. These were Gauguin's greatest works.

This self-portrait was painted on a door of a large wooden cupboard, when he was still in Brittany. It shows Gauguin with a halo over his head and a snake in his hand. Do you see the apple? Perhaps it reminds you of the Bible story of Adam and Eve. Gauguin may have portrayed himself as Adam after he had picked the forbidden fruit.

During his life as a painter, Gauguin was very poor and often sick. Fellow artists liked his paintings, but few people bought them. Only many years after his death was his talent appreciated. Now his paintings bring high prices.

## PAUL GAUGUIN
### *1848-1903*

*Paul Gauguin, Self-Portrait (1889); National Gallery of Art, Washington, D. C., Chester Dale Collection.*

*Vincent Van Gogh, Self-Portrait with Bandaged Ear (1889); Collection of Mr. & Mrs. Leigh B. Block, Chicago.*

# VINCENT VAN GOGH
## *1853-1890*

Vincent Van Gogh's brilliant, bold pictures painted with quick, heavy brush strokes give us no hint of his short and tragic life.

When he was 16, Van Gogh left his home in a small Dutch town and went to work as a salesman in his uncle's art gallery in The Hague. Van Gogh argued with the customers and his rudeness kept many away. Selling pictures just wasn't the job for this outspoken young man. Next he took a job as a teacher in a London boys' school, and in his spare time he studied the Bible. Van Gogh wanted to become a preacher. He prepared very carefully for the examinations to the ministry, but failed them. Very disappointed, he accepted a position as a missionary and was sent to a coal mining area in Belgium. The miners were so poor that Van Gogh gave them his food, clothes and money. They loved this ugly red-headed man who tried to give them hope. They called him "Christman." He sketched the miners as they worked, hoping to tell the world about their miseries. After two years, however, Van Gogh was dismissed. The authorities said his behavior was not proper for a missionary.

At this point, when he was 27 years old, Van Gogh knew that he would be an artist. Needing a rest and healthy food after his life with the miners, he went home to the peasant village where his father was a minister. Van Gogh had never gotten along well with his parents. They couldn't accept his strange behavior and ragged clothes. He was rude to the neighbors and argued with his father. He spent most of his time drawing the peasants as they dug potatoes in the fields and the weavers as they worked in their dark, damp huts. He painted these poor, sad and overworked people in dull browns and greys. Soon he left home again to travel to many places, painting and drawing wherever he went.

In Paris he made friends with the Impressionist painters. His style of painting changed. From the Impressionists he learned to put light and bright colors into his work. He studied Japanese art for its simplicity. When winter came to Paris, Van Gogh longed for a warmer place where he could paint out-of-doors in the bright sun.

He settled in Arles (arl), a small town in southern France. From sunrise to sunset he painted the beautiful countryside. He loved to paint the fruit trees blooming in the orchards, the cypress trees on the hills and the wheat waving in the fields. His energy was boundless. He worked quickly, brushing or squeezing thick colors directly out of the tube onto the canvas. Van Gogh liked to finish a painting at one sitting. Reds, blues and yellows, so different from the greys and browns of former days, made his paintings glow.

Van Gogh could seldom afford a model so he often painted himself. He painted 22 self-portraits. This one was painted in Arles during a period of mental illness. It was one of his last self-portraits. In a frenzy, after an argument with Gauguin, Van Gogh had cut off a piece of his ear. After a few days the wound felt better and he painted himself with a fur cap, pipe and bandaged ear. His deep-set blue eyes stare strangely at us and there is only a hint of his red beard. Do you see the characteristic heavy brush strokes that capture the fur cap and coat?

Van Gogh never fully recovered from this illness. He spent several months in a mental hospital. He was depressed, unsatisfied with his paintings, and in deep debt to his brother Theo. When he felt that he could no longer face his problems, he shot himself. Before his death he had sold only one of his more than 500 paintings. Today he is considered one of the greatest artists of his time.

# PAUL CEZANNE
## *1839-1906*

Paul Cezanne (say-zan) painted about 40 self-portraits. The earliest shows the painter when 20 years old, and the latest at about 60 years of age. The self-portrait pictured here was done in Paris when Cezanne was 38 years old. It is painted in the Impressionistic style.

Such a large number of self-portraits might make one think that Cezanne was a very vain or self-centered man. Actually, he painted whatever was close at hand—the landscape outside his door or objects he had around his house, such as a basket of fruit, a bunch of flowers or a bottle of wine. If he felt like painting a portrait, the model was his wife or son or anyone with enough patience to sit very still for many hours. "Do I have to tell you again," he would bark gruffly at a squirming model, "You must sit like an apple. Does an apple move?" The most patient model of all was himself, seen in a mirror. This model didn't fidget if the slow, methodical artist spent a whole day repainting a collar or hairline.

Most of Cezanne's Impressionistic paintings were misunderstood and laughed at. He became disgusted with life in Paris and returned to his hometown of Aix-en-Provence (ex-on-pruh-vahns) in southern France. There he stayed for 25 years, until his death.

He worked and experimented with Impressionism, trying to develop his own ideas from it. He said, "I want to make Impressionism something solid and permanent like the old masters."

He often walked in the woods, lugging his canvases and easel, until he found a good place to paint. Outdoors he could see the effects of the sun and clouds on the hills and trees.

Cezanne had an inheritance left by his father. He didn't have to worry about selling his work, and because he didn't have to please the public he had greater freedom to develop new styles of painting. Cezanne's ideas culminated in an exciting new idea which formed an important link between 19th century art and the modern art of the 20th century. Modern art grew out of Cezanne's realization that you can't put a chair, a person or a tree into a picture without changing it to fit the canvas.

Cezanne said, "Every shape in nature is based on the circle, the cone and the cylinder." This idea influenced artists like Picasso (pea-CAH-so) and Braque (brock) in developing *Cubism*. Cezanne's theories and his work earned him the title of "the father of modern art".

*Paul Cezanne, Self-Portrait (1877); The Phillips Collection, Washington, D. C.*

Pablo Picasso is considered by many as the most important and influential artist of our century. He is certainly one of the most famous. He is known for both his paintings and sculpture. His art shows many styles and moods—from Realism to Primitivism and from Classicism to Cubism.

The son of an artist, Picasso was born in Malaga, Spain. As a boy, he helped his father paint. He drew the difficult parts on his father's canvases, such as hands and feet. When Picasso was 14 his father realized his son's talents had surpassed his own. He gave his paints and brushes to his son saying he would never need them again.

Picasso moved to Paris at the age of 25. He wanted to be in the city where so many artists were working and so many artistic ideas were discussed. There he painted this bold self-portrait. It shows a serious young painter with his palette in hand. The look in the dark eyes of the short, stocky man is searching and remarkably alive. The portrait is painted in the greys and blues that are characteristics of Picasso's Blue Period. This early style is marked by tenderness and sensitivity.

A few years later Picasso and Georges Braque (1882-1963) developed a style of art called *Cubism*. Cubism was one of the important phases in the development of modern art. Cubism combines shapes and planes in an attempt to analyze what the artist sees. The Cubist takes a subject like a head and reduces it to many geometric shapes. He might paint the nose like a cone, the eyes like triangles and the cheeks like cubes.

Sometimes Picasso glued pieces of cloth, buttons, strings, newspaper and wood to a painting. These pictures were called *collages,* (coh-lahzh) from the French word *colle,* which means to glue.

Picasso is now aged, and wealthy from the sale of his art. He still works very hard. His paintings and sculpture continue to be original and imaginative. Recently he started to make pottery. Picasso enjoys having his young children look over his shoulder as he works.

## PABLO PICASSO
### *1881-*

Picasso
1906

*Henri Matisse, Self-Portrait (1906); State Museum of Art, Copenhagen.*

# HENRI MATISSE
## *1869-1954*

Henri Matisse (on-ree ma-TEESS) was called the "King of the Wild Beasts". The *Fauves* (foves), or Wild Beasts, was a name given by the public in 1905 to a group of French artists whose paintings they thought looked savage. Swishes of shocking colors were dashed wildly on the canvas. The Fauves didn't care too much about perspective or subject matter. They were mainly interested in the arrangement of color and shapes. They painted green haired women, purple horses and bright red trees. People were shocked. Today, we hardly comment because we are so used to this type of painting.

This self-portrait shows Matisse as a young bearded man. It is boldly painted in the striking style of the Fauves. Matisse wasn't interested in telling us how he looked, although we do see a rather strong, good-looking man. He wanted to show us how he felt. He often said . . . . "while working, I never try to think, only to feel". The bold strokes seem to say that Matisse had confidence in his painting.

As a young man, Matisse studied law. He started to paint to pass the time while recovering from an operation. Painting was so exciting and challenging that he decided to give up law and devote his full attention to art. In Paris he worked with several teachers and studied Impressionism and Oriental art. He was searching for the style that was right for him. Finally he and several other artists developed Fauvism. At first everyone laughed at them. It was very difficult for Matisse to sell enough paintings to support his family.

Slowly he perfected from Fauvism a personal, strong, decorative and unique style very dependent on bright color, and so simple that people said a child could do as well. To this remark Matisse would answer, "That is what I'm trying to do. I should like to recapture that freshness of vision which is characteristic of youth, when all the world is new...."

As the public came to accept modern art, Matisse's drawings and paintings were more readily understood. His work was valued and admired, and his influence was seen in the work of many contemporary artists. "We of today," he told a reporter, "are trying to express ourselves today—now—the 20th century—and not to copy what the Greeks saw and felt in art 2,000 years ago ..."

*Piet Mondrian, Self-Portrait (1918); Gemeente Museum, The Hague, on loan from S. B. Slijper collection.*

# PIET MONDRIAN
## *1872-1944*

The paintings of Piet Mondrian (peet MON-dree-ahn) look something like a new stream-lined office building constructed with rows and rows of glass windows held together by steel beams. Mondrian crossed his canvases with bold black horizontal and vertical lines, and filled in the resulting boxes with white, red, yellow or blue. He used color, line and shape for their own sake, without painting a scene or an object. This style of art is called *Non-representational.*

Mondrian didn't always paint in this style. He started out in his homeland of Holland painting realistic landscapes. While living in Paris, he became interested in the work of Picasso and the Cubists. Slowly, his unique Non-representational use of cubes and squares developed. Mondrian's new style pleased some critics and some of the public, but it didn't sell well.

This self-portrait is one of several done by the artist. It was painted about five years after he had developed his Non-representational style. A realistic painting like this portrait would indicate a giant step backwards. Actually, Mondrian painted this as a special favor for a friend who wouldn't buy any of his pictures of colored boxes. By painting squares and rectangles in the background you can see that he couldn't resist showing his current interest. Curiously, Mondrian signed this picture by spelling his name the way he had done when painting landscapes. In the left-hand corner of this painting you can see *Mondriaan* instead of the now common *Mondrian.*

The look on Mondrian's face is rather strange and mysterious. Looking at him, it is possible to believe the story that in a fit of rage he shot a canvas full of holes because he wasn't satisfied with a self-portrait he had painted on it.

Max Beckmann produced many self-portraits. He usually painted himself as a proper gentleman, wearing a business suit or formal evening dress. A man dressed in paint-spattered overalls and standing at an easel did not convey Beckmann's idea of how a successful artist should look.

This self-portrait was painted in Amsterdam. Beckmann had just settled there after fleeing from Nazi Germany. The man in this self-portrait is troubled and uncertain. He has lost his teaching position and home, and has known the horrors of Nazism.

Beckmann's portrait of himself is painted in the *Expressionist* style, a style that emerged in Germany during the first quarter of the 20th century. Expressionism *expresses,* or shows, the artist's feelings about himself and the world. In his work Beckmann expressed his bitterness about war and the unrest and despair of our civilization. Bright, bold colors, sharp contrasts, strong lines, drama and distortion are characteristics of Expressionism and are present in this self-portrait. Beckmann was one of the foremost Expressionists.

### MAX BECKMANN
*1884-1950*

*Max Beckmann, Self-Portrait (1937); The Art Institute of Chicago, gift of Mr. & Mrs. Philip Ringer.*

MARC CHAGALL
*1887-*

*Marc Chagall, Self-Portrait with a Wine Glass (1917);*
*Musee d'Art Moderne, Paris; Photo Giraudon.*

This is a happy self-portrait! Marc Chagall (shah-GAHL) rides piggy-back on his wife Bella's shoulders, smiling happily and holding a glass of wine. The sun is shining and an angel flies by. In Bella's hand is a fan, and at her feet is their hometown of Vitebsk, a little Russian village on the Dvina River. The colors in the picture are gay and bright. Chagall wears a vivid red jacket and his wife looks lovely in a long white dress and purple stockings. You might guess that this was their wedding picture, but the reason for this joyful portrait was the Chagalls' trip home to Vitebsk for a visit.

At the age of 23 Chagall had left Russia and moved to Paris to study and paint. Away from home, and lonely, Chagall dreamed of his family, the celebrations, the rabbis, the animals and peasants that were an important part of his early life. From his memory he painted scenes of weddings, musicians fiddling and rabbis praying, usually in front of small village houses. Some of these pictures seem to come from a colorful fairyland where donkeys fly, peddlers float over steeples and storytellers stand on their heads. These are highly individualistic pictures portraying the simple, religious, and sometimes tragic, life of the Jews of Vitebsk, as Chagall remembered and interpreted it with his lively imagination.

Chagall lives in France today. He is old, but is still active and busy as an artist. His work still has the childlike wonder and imagination it had back in 1917 when he produced one of the most lively self-portraits of our time.

## ABOUT THE AUTHOR

## ABOUT THE DESIGNER

Sharon Lerner is an artist, teacher and author. As an artist she prefers to paint in watercolors and make silver jewelry. She has a degree in art education from the University of Minnesota, and subsequently taught at the University High School, the White Bear Public School System, and the Walker Art Center. She has been a lecturer and guide at Walker, and The Minneapolis Institute of Arts. At present she is art director of Lerner Publications.

Robert Clark Nelson is a distinguished designer with extensive achievements to his credit. He is a graduate of the Minneapolis School of Arts and Bethel College, and is currently an instructor in art, painting and graphic design at the latter institution.

Mr. Nelson's work has been included in five editions of the *Graphic Annual*, and two editions of the *New York Art Directors Annual*. His most recent honor has been the inclusion of four of his posters in the *International Poster Annual*, a Swiss publication covering the poster art of 26 countries.